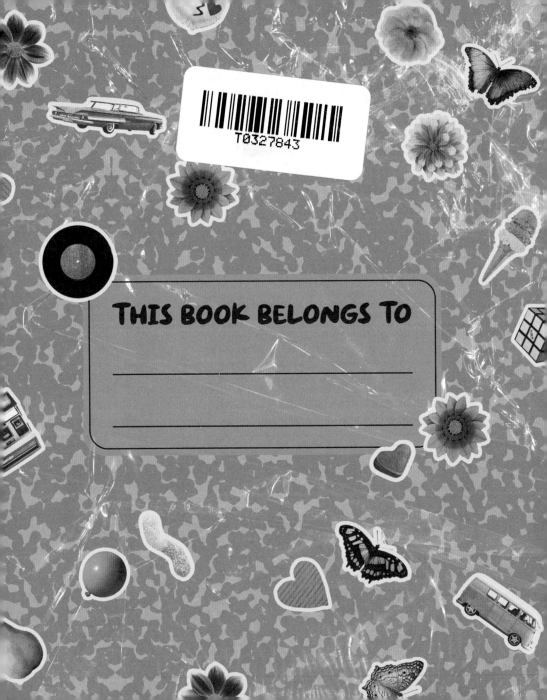

THIS BOOK BELONGS TO

_____

_____

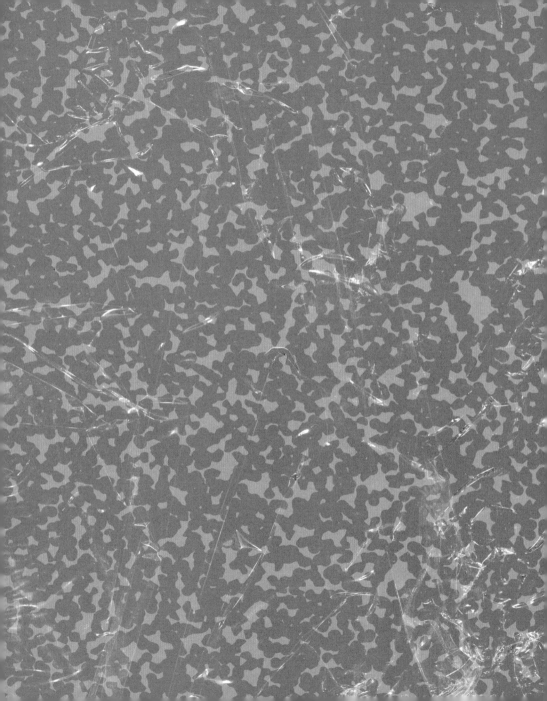

OLIVIA is a self-professed SWIFTIE.

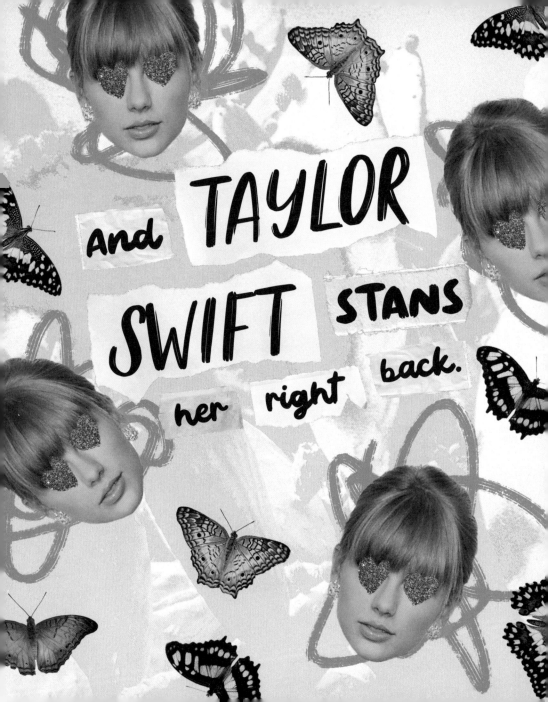

and TAYLOR SWIFT STANS her right back.

OLIVIA'S ALBUM "SOUR" was one of the very few'

GOOD THINGS

to happen to

the PLANET

in 2021.

OLIVIA negotiated with her record label to own the **MASTERS** of all her *music.* That's some **REAL CEO ENERGY.**

She's broken some SERIOUS spotify streaming records — she beat herself for the most plays in one week by EVER MILLIONS.

"I try to be as **HONEST** as I can **POSSIBLY BE.** All of my songs are about my experience **BEING** a teenager and **FIGURING** LIFE out."

you just
know there's
an EGOT
on her
HORIZON.

In her **first** **film,**

"AN AMERICAN GIRL:
GRACE STIRS UP SUCCESS",

olivia played **GRACE,**

a TALENTED baker.

It was the PERFECT RECIPE for on-screen SUCCESS.

WE OWE
olivia's mum
a debt of GRATITUDE.
she took young olivia
RECORD SHOPPING
and introduced
her to GRUNGE
and RIOT GRRRL.

olivia wrote HER FIRST song when she was JUST EIGHT years old.

"I remember playing it in my living room and hearing my Mom CRYING as she tried to pretend like she wasn't listening."

At 13, she played PAIGE IN DISNEY'S "Bizaardvark" and OMG AMBITION looks great ON HER.

"Technically it took me FOUR APPOINTMENTS and two attempts to complete my driver's test ...

I literally cried
in the DMV parking lot.
BUT when I finally got it
a couple months later,
I GOT A SONG OUT OF IT!"

she's a HUUUUGE NO DOUBT FAN,

which

just goes

to show she

has taste.

olivia has said she **LOVES** NOTHING MORE than cruising over to **MALIBU** for a swim and, **GIRL,** text me next time.

Hardcore fans haven't come to a **CONSENSUS** on how they should be known collectively,

but some
GREAT
-itches include
olives, Hot Rods,
DMV clerks,
Rodrigohoes and
Sour patch kids.

According to Sam Riback over at Olivia's label, "I've been doing this for a minute, and USUALLY what you hear from YOUNG WRITERS are parts of sonfs ... BUT with olivia it's the WHOLE COMPOSITION that's so well put together."

Like anyone born after 2000 with a pulse, Olivia grew up LIVING for TWILIGHT." She even wrote a song about THE MOMENT that Bella and Edward met in science class and their resulting... CHEMISTRY.

...he is **OBSESSED** with watching **JEOPARDY!"** and we need **TO KNOW** when that celebrity guest edition is happening.

"I really tried to REMEMBER that what OTHER PEOPLE SAY OR DO has NOTHING to do with me, and EVERYTHING to do with THEM. I think adopting THAT MINDSET has HELPED ME GET OVER a lot of INSECURITY and self doubt."

olivia really blew up when she starred as Nini in the Disney+ HIT, "High School Musical: The Series". If she's not in the next season, then we DON'T WANT IT.

she
HIGH KEY
went and
SNATCHED
three
GRAMMY
AWARDS
at 19 years old.

OLIVIA knows that the "TWILIGHT" OS is one of the GREATEST albums of all time.

She's on a REGULAR TEXTING BASIS with One Direction's NIALL HORAN. "He's giving me like advice on all THE CRAZINESS of the music industry. It's been really amazing." NO CAP.

Before her

DISNEY GLOW UP,

olivia wanted to be AN OLYMPIC GYMNAST.

"I was terrible at it - TERRIBLE!" she admits now. "But I was like 'MOM AND DAD, THIS IS WHAT WE'RE DOING.'"

In the early days of lockdown, Olivia set herself an ARTISTIC GOAL to write at least ONE VERSE and a CHORUS every damn DAY. And it worked. (For the first few months of the pandemic, anyway.)

she's the STRAIGHT-UP GOAT of lyrical vulnerability

"SNL" aired a sketch about "DRIVERS LICENSE,"

which
is when you know
you are the
ZEITGEIST.

ฝรั่ง

The first concert she ever went to was WEEZER,

THE OG

angsty

kings.

Olivia's most PRIZED POSSESSIONS are her American Girl Dolls, which is a whole MOOD when you own platinum stacks of records.

she's **DYING** to star in an

ACTION MOVIE and we will **MANIFEST** it for you, BESTIE.

OLIVIA is THE STYLE ICON of our moment. And a humble one

"I WOULD CALL IT 'I'M 18 and truly have no sense of personal style yet, BUT I TRY."

Olivia's

FAVORITE

thing to cook herself is

cacio e pepe. (IYKYK)

HER FAVORITE SNACK? "Trader Joe's oatmeal cookies till the day I die."

she gets
through long nights
in the studio
by knitting. CRAFT
GOALS, TBH.

Her go-to

ICEBREAKER?

Asking strangers if they have a good

GHOST STORY.

She was

once

GIFTED

aviators,   M&Ms,

and a shoe horn

by   JOE BIDEN.

YES,   that's right:

a presidential

shoe horn (!!??).

olivia's recieved

DATING ADVICE

from

ALANIS

MORRISETTE

and we'd
DIE TO KNOW
what Alanis told her.

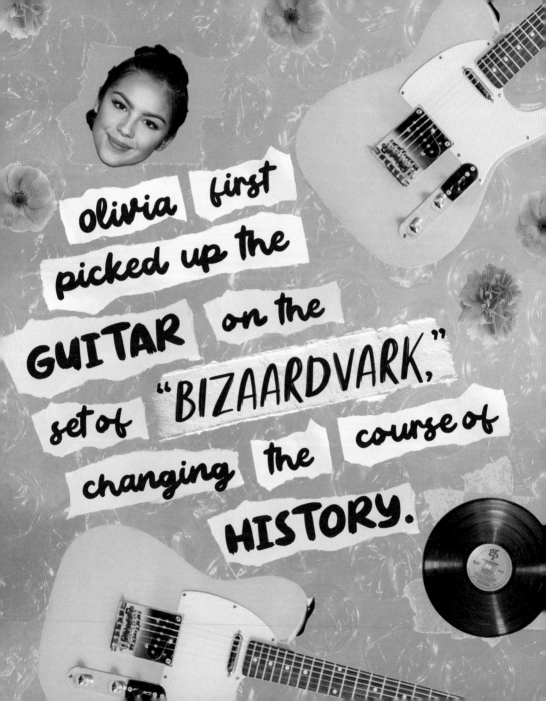

Olivia first picked up the GUITAR on the set of "BIZAARDVARK," changing the course of HISTORY.

When she's not keeping busy as the **NEW VOICE** of a generation, Olivia is a speaker and panelist for the Geena Davis Institute on Gender in Media.

she
identifies as a
"SPICY
PISCES."

Iconically, olivia used to write

she stands
on the SHOULDERS
of fellow
DISNEY ALUMN
and QUEEN.
OF POP,

BRITNEY
& ARIANA.

"All I want", a song she wrote for "High School Musical: The Musical: the series", was so POPULAR it placed on the BILLBOARD HOT 100 CHART.

Her first on screen work was for an **OLD NAVY** commercial that also featured FRED ARMISEN in drag. ICONIC.

when the supreme court overturned ROE v. WADE olivia brought LILY ALLEN on during her Glastonbury set to perform a pointed rendition of "F*CK YOU."

"you can't EMPOWER one woman in another country at the expense of another woman in another country. It doesn't make any sense to me."

OLIVIA is a certified TRIPLE THREAT–

she can SING, ACT and DANCE the house down.

PRODUCTION

DIRECTOR

CAMERA PERSON

OLIVIA has a SECRET VAULT of unreleased songs that might ACTUALLY break the internet when she CRACKS it open.

Smith Street Books

Published in 2023 by Smith Street Books
Naarm (Melbourne) | Australia
smithstreetbooks.com

ISBN: 978-1-9227-5443-1

All rights reserved. No part of this book may be reproduced or transmitted by any person or entity, in any form or by any means, electronic or mechanical, including photocopying, recording, scanning or by any storage and retrieval system, without the prior written permission of the publishers and copyright holders.

Copyright text & design © Smith Street Books
Copyright stock photography © alamy.com, shutterstock.com, unsplash.com

Publisher: Paul McNally
Project editor: Avery Hayes & Patrick Boyle
Design layout: George Saad & Brittney Griffiths
Proofreader: Hannah Koelmeyer

Printed & bound in China by C&C Offset Printing Co., Ltd.

Book 270
10 9 8 7 6 5 4 3 2 1

Please note: This title is not affiliated with or endorsed in any way by Olivia. We are just big fans. Please don't sue us.

MIX
Paper | Supporting responsible forestry
FSC® C008047

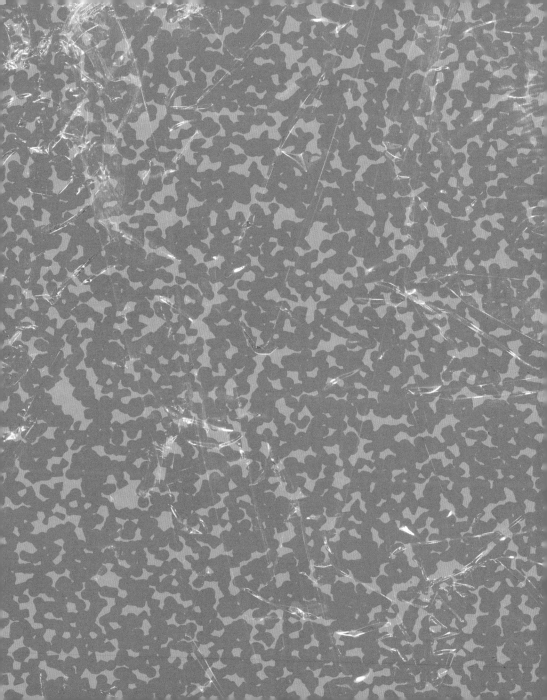

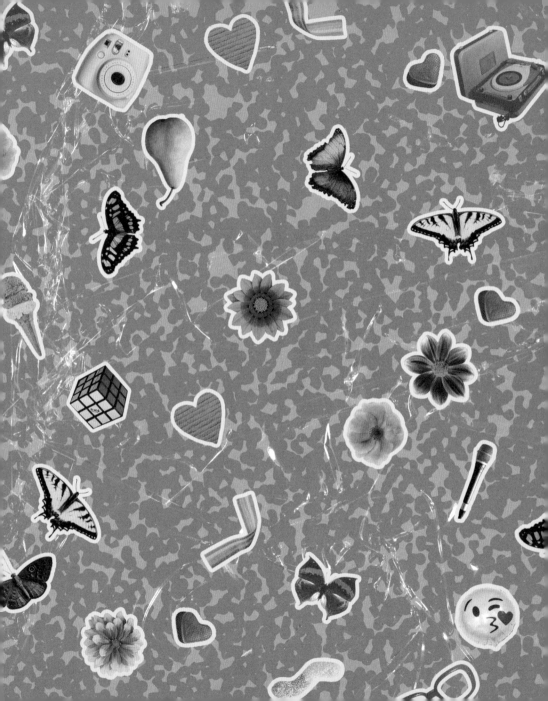